T0387391

EUROPE

by Catherine C. Finan

BEARPORT
PUBLISHING

Minneapolis, Minnesota

Bearport Publishing Company Product Development Team
President: Jen Jenson; Director of Product Development: Spencer Brinker; Managing Editor: Allison Juda; Associate Editor: Naomi Reich; Associate Editor: Tiana Tran; Art Director: Colin O'Dea; Designer: Elena Klinkner; Designer: Kayla Eggert; Product Development Assistant: Owen Hamlin

Produced for Bearport Publishing by BlueAppleWorks Inc.
Managing Editor for BlueAppleWorks: Melissa McClellan; Art Director: T.J. Choleva; Photo Research: Jane Reid

STATEMENT ON USAGE OF GENERATIVE ARTIFICIAL INTELLIGENCE
Bearport Publishing remains committed to publishing high-quality nonfiction books. Therefore, we restrict the use of generative AI to ensure accuracy of all text and visual components pertaining to a book's subject. See BearportPublishing.com for details.

Library of Congress Cataloging-in-Publication Data

Names: Finan, Catherine C., 1972- author.
Title: Europe / by Catherine C. Finan.
Description: Minneapolis, Minnesota : Bearport Publishing Company, [2024] | Series: X-treme facts : continents | Includes bibliographical references and index.
Identifiers: LCCN 2023032035 (print) | LCCN 2023032036 (ebook) | ISBN 9798889164333 (hardcover) | ISBN 9798889164418 (paperback) | ISBN 9798889164487 (ebook)
Subjects: LCSH: Europe--Juvenile literature.
Classification: LCC D1051 .F55 2024 (print) | LCC D1051 (ebook) | DDC 940--dc23/eng/20230719
LC record available at https://lccn.loc.gov/2023032035
LC ebook record available at https://lccn.loc.gov/2023032036

For more information, write to Bearport Publishing, 5357 Penn Avenue South, Minneapolis, MN 55419.

Contents

Welcome to Europe!

Have you ever dreamed of visiting the bustling streets of Paris, France, or roaming the ancient ruins of Rome, Italy? Maybe your ideal adventure has you skiing down a mountain, sailing on the sea, or exploring cool castles. You can do all of these things and more in Europe! We're taking a trip to Earth's second-smallest **continent**, a fantastic region known for its beautiful landscapes, fascinating history, and many amazing cultures. Let the journey begin!

Northern parts of the continent lie above the freezing Arctic Circle, but **temperatures are much warmer in southern Europe along the Mediterranean Sea.**

Arctic Circle

ASIA

Atlantic Ocean

Ural Mountains

EUROPE

Mediterranean Sea

Europe ends at the Atlantic Ocean in the west and the Ural Mountains on its eastern edge.

The continent is made up of 50 different nations. Some, including Turkey, are part of both Europe and Asia.

EVERYBODY HERE SPEAKS A DIFFERENT LANGUAGE. HOW WILL WE GET DIRECTIONS?

WE'RE BOUND TO FIND SOMEONE WHO SPEAKS THE SAME LANGUAGE AS US.

About 200 languages are spoken in Europe.

At less than a quarter of a square mile (half a sq km), **Vatican City is the world's smallest country. It's inside Rome.**

EUROPE IS SO BEAUTIFUL!

YEAH, IT HAS A LITTLE BIT OF EVERYTHING!

Europe has many different landscapes, from rugged fjords and jagged mountain peaks to lush fields and rolling forests.

A Very Long History

Europe has a long history. It's thought that people may have first appeared on the continent more than 200,000 years ago. The first European **civilization** started almost 5,000 years ago in present-day Greece. The ancient Greeks had many ideas about art, **philosophy**, and government. These ideas **influenced** later Europeans, including the ancient Romans. Their civilization began 2,800 years ago and covered a huge part of the world for 700 years. It's time for a quick European history lesson!

The Roman Empire fell in 476 CE. **Much of ancient Rome's culture was lost during the Middle Ages that followed.**

The Middle Ages are sometimes called the Dark Ages because there were many wars, diseases, and **famines**.

The Middle Ages spanned from about 500 CE to 1400 CE. During this time, wealthy people owned the land and ruled over the farmers who worked it.

During the mid-1300s, a disease called the Black Death killed millions of people. It was spread by the bites of **infected** fleas carried by rats.

Next, came a period called the Renaissance which lasted until about the 1600s. This time is known for a rediscovery of art and philosophy.

The Renaissance gave us many inventions that changed our world, such as the printing press, telescopes, eyeglasses, and even ice cream!

The Industrial Revolution began in the 1700s. **Many people moved from the countryside to cities to work in factories.**

All Kinds of Climates

Throughout Europe's long history, its variety of climates has influenced how people in different regions have lived. The Scandinavian countries in the north have a cool, sometimes freezing climate. Most of the people there live in the area's cities, which were built in places where the weather isn't as extreme. In southern Europe, the climate is much warmer. Daily life in Italy, Spain, and Greece sometimes includes a midday break to beat the heat.

Countries across Europe experience the four seasons.

Europe's coldest temperature ever recorded was in Ust'-Shchugerr, Russia, **with a chilly −73 degrees Fahrenheit (−58 degrees Celsius).**

The Atlantic Ocean's warm winds give much of Europe a mild, rainy climate that's good for farming. Tulips are a famous crop from the Netherlands.

Grab your umbrella! **The United Kingdom gets up to 55 inches (140 cm) of rain per year.**

LET'S GO HOME. IT'S RAINING CATS AND DOGS.

WHERE? I WANT TO MAKE NEW FRIENDS!

Europe also has rain forests! The Perućica rain forest can be found in Bosnia and Herzegovina. **The Białowieża Forest stretches along the border of Poland and Belarus.**

The warm, dry climate around the Mediterranean Sea is great for olive trees. Spain, Italy, and Greece are the continent's top olive growers.

HOW MUCH OIL CAN WE GET FROM THESE OLIVES?

MAYBE A SPOONFUL!

It takes 50 to 200 pounds (20 to 90 kg) of olives to make about 1 gallon (4 L) of olive oil.

See the Seas

From the Mediterranean Sea in the south to the Baltic and North Seas on the other end of the continent, mighty bodies of water have long shaped life in Europe. Millions of people throughout the continent have relied on these wonderful waters for everything from food to travel. Jump aboard—it's time for a European sea extravaganza!

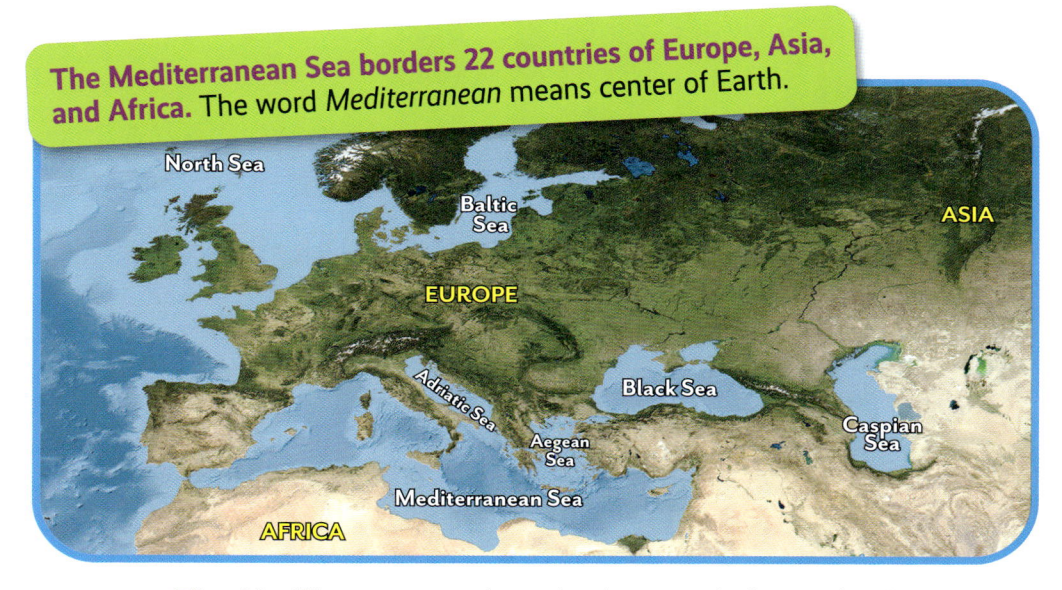

The Mediterranean Sea borders 22 countries of Europe, Asia, and Africa. The word *Mediterranean* means center of Earth.

The Mediterranean played a huge role in ancient trade routes. People from all over used the waterway to trade goods and knowledge.

The Mediterranean includes some smaller bodies of water. **The Adriatic Sea borders several countries, including Italy, Slovenia, and Croatia.**

Some people say eastern Europe's Caspian Sea is actually a lake, since it's a landlocked body of water that doesn't feed into an ocean.

The North Sea borders several northern European countries. The area's stormy conditions, winter fog, and strong currents make it one of Earth's most dangerous seas.

The Black Sea lies where Europe and Asia meet. There, scientists have discovered the world's oldest shipwreck—from about 2,400 years ago!

The Aegean Sea, also part of the Mediterranean, sits between Greece and Turkey. It's believed people explored it 15,000 years ago!

Marvelous Mountains

Let's explore Europe's marvelous mountains. Perhaps the most well-known are the Alps. This range stretches for 750 miles (1,200 km) through 8 countries. But these aren't the only peaks Europe has to offer. The Pyrenees Mountains form a 270-mile (430-km) wall between France and Spain. Along Europe's easternmost border, the Ural Mountains span from the Arctic Ocean to Kazakhstan. And the crescent-shaped Carpathian range extends through several countries, including Slovakia and Romania.

The tiny country of Andorra is hidden in the Pyrenees. At just 180 square miles (470 sq km), this country is smaller than the city of Scottsdale, Arizona.

WHAT A GREAT PEAK!

YOU'RE TELLING ME! I CAN PEEK AT ALL THE MEADOWS FROM HERE.

One of Europe's most famous mountains is the Matterhorn in the Alps. It rises nearly 14,700 feet (4,500 m) above the border between Switzerland and Italy.

The name *Matterhorn* comes from the German word meaning the peak in the meadows.

Europe's highest peak, Mount Elbrus, is part of the Caucasus Range in Russia. It's actually an inactive volcano.

REAL OR NOT, I'M NOT TAKING RISKS WITH VAMPIRES!

Bran Castle is nestled in the Carpathian Mountains in Romania. It's sometimes called Dracula's Castle, named after the famous fictional vampire.

The Ural Mountains in Russia are between 250 and 300 million years old, **making them one of the oldest ranges on the planet.**

HEY ZEUS, DO YOU THINK YOU COULD FIND A PLACE WITH BETTER VIEWS.

PROBABLY NOT. THIS IS THE TALLEST MOUNTAIN AROUND!

Mount Olympus is Greece's tallest mountain. In Greek mythology, this peak was the home of the gods.

Remarkable Rivers, Cool Canals

Europe's mountains are majestic and its seas are sensational, but the continent also has many famous rivers and **canals**. For thousands of years, Europeans have traveled from place to place using rivers. To this day, people from around the world visit Europe to cruise its rivers and canals and enjoy the continent's beautiful sights from the water.

The continent's second-longest river, the Danube, flows through 10 different countries. That's quite a voyage!

More than 200 bridges span England's river Thames. The river provides the people of London with about 80 percent of their drinking water.

WHERE DO YOU THINK THE RIVER BEGINS?

WE COULD SWIM IT TO FIND OUT.

Flowing for more than 2,200 miles (3,500 km), the Volga is Europe's longest river. Surprisingly, its source is a small stream flowing from a swamp!

The Rhine flows through six countries, including Austria, France, and the Netherlands. The river is called a different name in each of these places.

Amsterdam in the Netherlands has 60 miles (100 km) of canals running between the city's 90 different islands. **Some people live in houseboats on these canals!**

Venice, Italy, is famous for its beautiful canals. People take boats through the waterways to get around.

Outstanding Islands

With so much water, is it any wonder that many European countries are famous for their incredible islands? Italy's Sicily, Greece's Santorini, and France's Corsica are all popular vacation destinations. Some islands are actually entire countries! The island nations of Iceland, Ireland, and Great Britain are surrounded on all sides by the Atlantic Ocean. The Mediterranean Sea is home to the island countries of Cyprus and Malta.

Great Britain is Europe's largest island. It includes the countries of England, Wales, and Scotland.

WHAT HAVE YOU PEOPLE DONE WITH MY ICELAND?!

IT'S CALLED PROGRESS, OLD-TIMER!

Iceland's unique landscape features hot springs and volcanoes. Perhaps even cooler, the country was founded by **Vikings!**

The French island of Corsica is covered in fragrant plants, including lavender, sage, and rosemary. It's nicknamed the Scented Isle.

EVERYTHING SMELLS SO GREAT AROUND HERE!

Santorini's white buildings are beautiful and useful. **The white paint reflects sunlight to help keep homes cool on the hot island.**

Sicily is home to Europe's tallest and most active volcano, Mount Etna. The volcano has been active for more than two million years.

WOW! THAT WATER IS SO BLUE.

WELL, IT IS THE BLUE LAGOON!

Care to relax? Malta's Blue **Lagoon** has beautiful waters and rugged cliffs.

Europe's Unique Animals

Many unique animals call Europe's **diverse** habitats home. In the far north, polar bears roam the Arctic lands. Throughout the continent's forests, brown bears and gray wolves live among the trees. You might even spy a spotted wildcat called a lynx in one of the mountain ranges. And adorable puffins perch on cliffs along the Atlantic shores of England, Scotland, and Ireland. Let's meet the animals!

Puffins can fly up to 55 miles per hour (90 kph). That's as fast as a car on some highways.

Wolverines can smell a dead animal buried more than 10 ft (3 m) deep in snow.

THE AIR IS SO COLD, IT'S HARD TO BREATHE!

YOU NEED AN AIR WARMER LIKE MINE.

The saiga is a kind of antelope with a unique nose. **Its special sniffer may help warm up cold winter air as it breathes in.**

Pine martens are named for the pine forests they call home. They mark their **territory** with their poop!

The chamois (sha-mee) is a goatlike animal found in the mountains. It can travel nearly 20 ft (6 m) in a single jump.

Reindeer spend almost half their lives in snow. The hollow hairs of their fur trap heat to keep the animals warm.

LET'S GO FOR A SWIM AFTER OUR RUN.

I THINK WE'LL HAVE TO WAIT FOR SPRING TO DO THAT!

The hollow hairs also help reindeer float, making them excellent swimmers!

Scenic Cities

From awe-inspiring nature to spectacular cities, there's so much to explore in Europe. In fact, hundreds of millions of people travel to the continent's many cities each year. There, they experience all the history, art, and delicious foods that countries across Europe have to offer. When planning a European city tour, it can be difficult to narrow down your list of choices!

Located just below the Arctic Circle, **Reykjavík, Iceland, is Europe's northernmost capital city.**

Each year, more than $1,000,000 worth of coins are thrown into the Trevi Fountain in Rome.

Zoom around London in a double-decker bus. Each year, the city's buses **drive a combined distance of about 300 million miles (480 million km).**

Tunnels beneath the streets of Paris hold the bones of millions of people in an elaborate underground cemetery!

Charles Bridge in Prague, Czech Republic, is said to be haunted.

Istanbul, Turkey's largest city, spans two continents. A channel of water called the Bosporus Strait divides the European and Asian parts of the city.

Let's Go Sightseeing

There are famous landmarks around every turn in Europe's incredible cities and towns. Visit the Colosseum in Rome, where **gladiators** fought one another thousands of years ago. In Athens, Greece, you can view the 2,500-year-old Parthenon, a temple built for the goddess Athena. In Moscow, Russia, the colorful onion-shaped domes of St. Basil's **Cathedral** loom large above the streets. And that's just the start!

When the Eiffel Tower in Paris was built in 1889, many people from the city hated it. Today, it's a famous landmark!

Some landmarks are modern, such as the Shard in London. The building was made to look like a sharp piece of glass.

WHAT A GREAT TOWER! LET'S GO TO THE TOP!

ONLY IF WE CAN TAKE THE ELEVATOR.

London's famous clock tower, often called Big Ben, is about 315 ft (95 m) tall. There are 399 steps to the top.

Neuschwanstein Castle in Germany may have been the inspiration for the famous castles in Disney World and Disneyland.

Some of the famous windmills in the Netherlands are hundreds of years old. They were built to use wind power to grind grain.

A tower in Pisa, Italy, started leaning before it was even completed. To this day, the Leaning Tower of Pisa is still crooked!

Meet the People

It's no surprise that among Europe's 750 million people, there is a wide variety of cultures and lifestyles. While many people live in cities, others make their homes throughout the countryside. In northern Europe, the Sámi people follow the ancient tradition of herding reindeer. Many southern Europeans make their living farming warm-weather crops. From north to south and east to west, there is so much to learn about the continent's amazing people.

TIME TO GO, AGAIN.

BUT I JUST LEARNED WHERE EVERYTHING IS!

The Sámi people move with their reindeer herds during the animals' winter migration.

It's believed Europe has about 160 different cultural groups. That's a whole lot of culture!

In Germany, the Sorb people are known for their beautifully decorated Easter eggs.

The Roma people reached eastern Europe from India in the 1300s. **Southern Spain's famous flamenco music and dance are based on Roma traditions.**

Most Europeans speak languages that fall into three main groups—**Romance, Germanic, and Slavic languages.**

Do you know any Spanish, French, or Italian words? **If so, you know a Romance language!**

CAN YOU SAY ANYTHING IN SPANISH?

¡HOLA!

WOW, I DIDN'T KNOW YOU SPOKE ROMANCE LANGUAGES!

WHAT'S SO DIFFERENT ABOUT THE EUSKARA LANGUAGE?

IT'S LIKE NOTHING YOU'VE EVER HEARD BEFORE.

The Basque people of the Pyrenees region speak Euskara. The language is unlike any other language in Europe.

Only in Europe

From its awesome animals and lovely landscapes to its captivating history and wonderful cultures, we've covered a lot of ground—literally! But there are many more fun facts to learn about this supercool continent. For example, its smallest town is Hum, Croatia, which has a population of just 30 people. And Europe's highest toilet sits atop France's Mont Blanc in the Alps, almost 14,000 ft (4,000 m) above sea level. Europe is certainly full of extremes!

Don't like mosquitos? **Consider moving to Iceland, where there aren't any.**

Belgium is famous for its chocolate. More chocolate is bought at the airport in the capital of Brussels than anywhere else in the world.

If you don't like to mow your lawn, you might want to move to Switzerland—**it's illegal to mow on Sundays there.**

TURN OFF THAT LAWN MOWER! IT'S SUNDAY!

WHAT'S WRONG, OFFICER?

A town in Wales has a name that is 58 letters long—that's quite a mouthful.

LLANFAIRPWLLGWYNGYLLGOGERYCHWYRNDROBWLLLLANTYSILIOGOGOGOCH

Llan-vire-pooll-guin-gill-go-ger-u-queern-drob-ooll-llandus-ilio-gogo-goch

WHERE ARE WE?

I DON'T KNOW. BUT WE'RE DEFINITELY NOT IN WALES!

Some towns in Denmark, Norway, and Sweden have names that are just one letter long.

Norway made a penguin at Scotland's Edinburgh Zoo a knight!

DID YOU HEAR NILS OLAV BECAME A KNIGHT?

I THOUGHT HE WAS A PENGUIN!

Make a Windmill

Craft Project

Windmills are found in many countries across Europe. They were first used to get power from nature. When a windmill's blades spun in the breeze, they worked machines that ground grain or pumped water. Make your own mini windmill.

In the Netherlands, there are 19 windmills that are 300 years old and still work!

What You Will Need

- A ruler
- Scissors
- Construction paper
- Glue
- A paper cup
- A paper fastener

Today, we use a modern type of windmill called a wind turbine to make electricity.

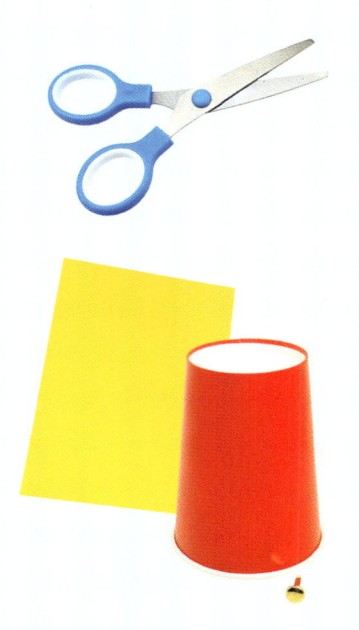

Step One

Cut two strips of construction paper, about 1 inch (2.5 cm) wide and slightly longer than the height of your cup.

Step Two

Cut a small rectangle of construction paper for a door. Flip the cup opening-side down, and glue the door to what is now the bottom of the cup.

Step Three

Overlap the two strips of paper together to make a plus sign, and glue them like that. These will be your blades.

Step Four

Poke the paper fastener through the center of the blades. Twist the fastener around a little to make the hole wider. The blades should be able to spin loosely on the fastener.

Step Five

Attach the paper blades above the door near the top of the cup. Open the fastener to secure the blades, but leave them a little loose. Your windmill is complete!

29

Glossary

canals narrow waterways used by boats traveling from place to place

cathedral a large, important church

civilization a large group of people that share the same history and way of life

continent one of Earth's seven large landmasses

diverse varied

famines times when there is a shortage of food

fjords long, narrow ocean passages between steep cliffs

gladiators men in ancient Rome who fought one another and wild animals to entertain others

infected full of harmful germs that make people sick

influenced had an affect on a person or thing

lagoon a shallow body of water separated from a larger body of water by a small piece of land

migration the movement of animals from one area to another at a certain time of year

mythology a collection of stories told by people to explain a practice, belief, or natural event

philosophy the study of the nature of life, truth, knowledge, and ways of thinking

territory an area that is marked and defended by an animal

Vikings a group of warriors from Norway, Denmark, and Sweden who lived from around 700 CE to about 1100 CE

Read More

Findlay, Galadriel. *Europe (Exploring Continents).* New York: Lightbox Learning Inc., 2023.

Harris, Tim. *Wildlife Worlds Europe (Wildlife Worlds).* New York: Crabtree Publishing Company, 2020.

Vonder Brink, Tracy. *Europe (Seven Continents of the World).* New York: Crabtree Publishing Company, 2023.

Learn More Online

1. Go to **www.factsurfer.com** or scan the QR code below.

2. Enter **"X-treme Europe"** into the search box.

3. Click on the cover of this book to see a list of websites.

Index

About the Author

Catherine C. Finan is a writer living in northeastern Pennsylvania. Her favorite European travel memory is watching the sunset in Santorini, Greece.